# Skateboarding Takes Shape

### by Loretta West

 HOUGHTON MIFFLIN    BOSTON

ILLUSTRATION CREDIT
Barry Gott

PHOTOGRAPHY CREDITS
**Cover** © Bob Shanley/Zuma Press; **1** © Corbis; **2** © Lambert/Hulton Archive/Getty Images; **10** © Davis Barber/PhotoEdit; **11** © Evan Hurd/Corbis

Copyright © by Houghton Mifflin Company. All rights reserved.

No part of this work may be reproduced or transmitted in any form or by any means, electronic or mechanical, including photocopying or recording, or by any information storage or retrieval system without the prior written permission of Houghton Mifflin Company unless such copying is expressly permitted by federal copyright law. Address inquiries to School Permissions, Houghton Mifflin Company, 222 Berkeley Street, Boston, MA 02116.

Printed in China

ISBN 10:  0-618-89997-9
ISBN 13:  978-0-618-89997-5

91011 0940 16 15 14 13
4500411355

# Surfers to Skateboarders

Imagine racing down a steep hill while balancing on nothing more than a board with four wheels. Sound like fun? The very first skateboarders thought so!

The sport of skateboarding began in Southern California in the 1950s.

The first skateboarders were called "sidewalk surfers." They were surfers with a problem. They needed something fun to do when the ocean was calm and they couldn't surf.

The goal of these "sidewalk surfers" was to create the same thrills and chills on land as they found in the ocean. So they'd start at the top of a hill and ride down on their homemade skateboards. They mostly hoped to stay on their boards and make it to the bottom without crashing into anything— like a car, a tree, or another skateboarder!

By the 1970s skateboarding was very popular. Because there were so many skateboarders in the United States, it made sense that they would want a special place to perform their stunts. They wanted a place to skate where they wouldn't have to worry about broken sidewalks and busy streets.

Skateparks are the perfect solution! Skateparks provide skateboarders with a safe, and yet exciting place to skateboard. Most skateparks have a variety of ramps. They have small, gently angled ramps for beginners. And they have steeper and more challenging ramps for experienced skaters.

Skateparks use angles like these to create ramps. They are both acute angles because they are less than 90°. A smaller angle makes a perfect ramp for beginning skateboarders.

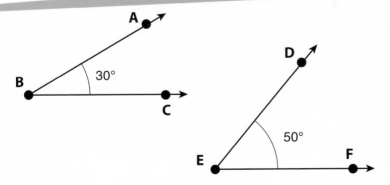

**Read·Think·Write** Which is the smaller angle? Which is the steeper angle?

# Special Places to Skateboard

You probably don't even realize it, but most of the ramps, rails, and platforms found in a skatepark are based on geometric shapes. Look at the picture. A triangle is a three-sided shape. A rectangle is a four-sided shape. Ramps are made by combining triangles and rectangles. Circles are also used in skateparks. Half-pipes and quarter-pipes are formed by using parts of a circle.

**Read·Think·Write** How many triangles do you see? How many rectangles do you see?

Parallel lines can also be seen in any skatepark. Parallel lines are always the same distance apart, and they never cross. They are different from intersecting lines, which do cross each other. Parallel lines are also different from perpendicular lines, which meet to form a right angle. By using these different lines, a skatepark can offer skateboarders a number of places to skateboard, such as rails, benches, and grind boxes.

# For Beginners

Let's take a closer look at the kinds of ramps a beginning skateboarder might use.

This is a launcher ramp. It's about 3 feet high, 4 feet wide, and 7 feet long. It's not very steep, but it's steep enough to get you started.

**Read·Think·Write** What geometric shapes make up a launcher ramp?

This ramp is called a quarter-pipe. It's rounded like part of a circle.

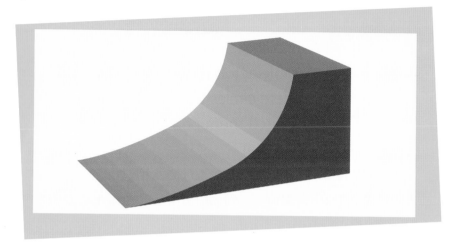

This is called a grind box. It can be used to join a launcher ramp and a quarter pipe. Or it can be used alone to practice leaps and jumps.

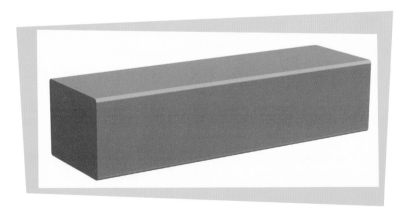

**Read·Think·Write**  What geometric shapes make up a grind box?

## More Advanced

Like all athletes, skateboarders have to practice, practice, and keep practicing some more to be able to leap and flip over obstacles. Some skateboarders are so good that they resemble acrobats as they fly through the air, making complete circles while still attached to their boards. As you watch them perform you might even think: How did they do that?

As much as their stunts have to do with balance, they also have to do with the kinds of ramps skateboarders use. One of the ramps a more experienced skateboarder might use is a half-pipe.

Several ramps can be put together to make a funbox. A funbox element is made of different polygons. A polygon is a shape with three or more sides. So triangles and rectangles are also polygons. Take a close look. A rectangular platform and a triangular ramp together make a polygon.

**Read·Think·Write**  How many polygons do you see?

# Twist, Turn, and Sail Through the Air!

It's pretty amazing what a person can do with a skateboard and a few ramps, isn't it? Since the first "sidewalk surfers," skateboarders have pushed the limit on using ramps, rails, and half-pipes.

Alan "Ollie" Gelfand invented the ollie in 1978. The ollie has become one of the most common stunts in skateboarding.

Lyn-Z Adams Hawkins started skateboarding when she was very young. She wanted to be like her big brother. At the age of thirteen, Lyn-Z won silver and bronze medals at the 2003 *X Games*. She went on to win another silver medal at the 2005 *X Games*.

Look at the skateboarders and their skateboards to answer the following questions.

1. Which skateboarder is skating on a ramp that has a rectangular top?

2. Which skateboarder is performing a stunt on a ramp that looks like a half-circle?

3. Which skateboarder's arms are parallel with the skateboard?

**A**          **B**          **C**

## Activity

Visualize  Draw your own skatepark or funbox. Include at least one triangle, one rectangle, and a set of parallel lines. Label each of these in your drawing.